THE BOOK LOVER'S JOKE BOOK

PRINTING OFFICE

REDDELL, BOOKSELLER & STATIONER

PATENT MEDICINE STAMPS PERFUMERY TOYS

No. 7 High Street TEWKESBUR

ALEX JOHNSON

THE BOOK LOVER'S JOKE BOOK

I slipped over in the library this morning. It was the non-friction section.

BRITISH LIBRARY

To Phyllis and Philip,
Wilma, Edward, Thomas and Robert

First published in Great Britain 2022 by
The British Library
96 Euston Road
London NW1 2DB

ISBN 978 0 7123 5451 6

British Library Cataloguing in Publication Data
A catalogue record for this publication is available from the
British Library

Designed by Georgie Hewitt
Printed in the Czech Republic by Finidr

Contents

Introduction

When I asked The British Library if they'd like to publish a collection of book jokes they actually suggested that I write a book on librarians. But I said no, because writing on paper is much easier. Eventually I convinced them and started working on the first draft on my laptop in the pub round the corner, but then the barman saw me and threw me out, shouting: "We don't want your typing here."

That's as good as it gets folks. I wouldn't blame you if you put the book straight back on the shelf right now. If you've already bought it and are reading it at home, apologies, but also thank you for funding my international playboy jetsetting lifestyle. My butler salutes you.

If you do carry on reading, you'll find jokes about books, writers, agents, publishers, librarians (the British Library are nothing if not persistent), grammar, bookcases, and cats. There are rib-ticklers for typographers, crackers for critics, and badly foxed quips about antiquarian bookshops. There's also more hilarity about the Lancashire County Council's mobile library vans than you'll find in any other book ever published. Fact.

In short, there is a good cross-section of the stuff that my wife and children have to put up with on a daily basis. Some of these jokes are great, some are pretty rubbish, and there are a couple which will make you go 'Eh?'. That one about Beatrix Potter is in here too.

What you won't find is pages and pages of smart-arse witticisms from Oscar Wilde (though I always enjoy rereading *The Picture of Dorian Gray* – never gets old), no 'hilarious puns' from Shakespeare's plays, no quotes from PG Wodehouse (actually, there is one, but it's a book dedication so I'm not counting that). On the other hand there is a great Dylan Thomas light bulb gag that's worth the price of the book in itself, and one about phrasebooks that's guaranteed to make you both smile and groan. In fact nearly everything on the following pages will make you do that, though not necessarily in that order.

Here too are the best literary April Fool's (the joke's on you), rejection letters (the joke's on the publisher), and Billy Wilder's tombstone (the joke's on him). The oldest joke dates back to the 4th century AD and I should warn you that there are some fakes here too.

On which note, it only remains for me to thank my editor Pru Freeder and my agent Paige Turner for their help in putting this book together. Any mistakes that you find in the following pages are of course all theirs.

Alex Johnson

Ca.lrrij.

Animals

Why did the chicken turn the page?
To get to the other side.

My cousin is a successful writer of novels about marine life.
Everybody likes his polyp fiction.

I'm working hard on an early version of my book on dog
linguistics.
It's a ruff draft.

A man sees a badger sitting a few seats away from him in the
cinema eating a hot dog and asks "What are you doing here?"
The badger says: "Well, I liked the book so I wanted to see what
the film was like."

Why don't rabbits like sad books?
They prefer ones with hoppy endings.

Why did the dog sprint after the book?
He was chasing his tale.

A polyp or octopus
from the *Hortus
Sanitatis* (The
Garden of Health)
natural history
encyclopedia
published by Jacob
Meydenbach in
Mainz (1491).

April Fool's

American magazine *The Saturday Review* featured an article about 5th-century BC grammarian Kohmar Pehriad who advocated the use of the full stop and who provided the inspiration for the comma. His son, Apos-Trophe Pehriad, was also evangelical about punctuation marks.

Radio Carlisle revealed that William Wordsworth's Dove Cottage home in the Lake District had been sold to an American who was intending to dismantle it brick by brick and rebuild it in Arizona.

The Times disclosed that it had been shown original papers written by Sherlock Holmes that he had invented Moriarty to annoy Dr Watson.

A paper in science journal *Nature* claimed a dinosaur skeleton had been discovered by Randy Sepulchrave from the little

"HOLMES PULLED OUT HIS WATCH."

known University of Southern North Dakota
who believed that not only was it was able to
fly, but it had a kind of flexible body armour
and ribs which appeared to be charred by fire.
It had been named Smaugia Volans (of interest
to readers of *The Hobbit*) by Sepulchrave (co-
incidentally the name of the owl-obsessed 76th
Earl of Groan in Mervyn Peake's *Titus Groan*).

2001

The Observer focused on plans by a dot.com entrepreneur
to build a Cybrary, a bricks-and-mortar building which would

hold printouts of all the books currently available online on the internet.

2010

The Today programme on BBC Radio 4 reported that a newly discovered locket revealed William Shakespeare was French.

2012

The British Library came across a mid-14th-century cookbook by Geoffrey Fule in its archives with a recipe for unicorns, including a picture of a unicorn on the grill. The book apparently also included recipes for tripe and codswallop.

A golden miniature of a unicorn from a medieval bestiary produced in England in the 2nd quarter of the 13th century.

Coming soon...

How To Read by Abe E Seas

How To Read II by Al Fabbette

The Crime of the Century by Mr E

The Case of the Blank Book by MT Pages

Basic Subediting by Tye Poe

The Book of Long Books by Warren Piece

How To Write Suspense Stories by Paige Turner

2013

Kevin Merden, Director of Tissue Buying at Asda, announced the supermarket would soon be producing *Fifty Shades of Grey* toilet paper on the back of EL James's bestselling book success.

2015

The Paris Review scooped the world with an interview with Eric Carle in which he revealed that he had fought bitterly with his publishers over the inclusion of the stomach ache scene in *The Hungry Caterpillar* which they demanded be included as punishment for overeating. This 'scoop' resurfaced widely online on Carle's death in 2021.

Authors

What do you do with a famous novelist at the launch party of their new book?
Roll out the read carpet.

I've got this great Cormac McCarthy joke but it doesn't have quotation marks so some people can't tell the difference between when the people in my joke are talking and when I'm talking as the joke's narrator.

Why is your copy of 'The Raven' soaking wet?
Well, you told me to dip my Poe in the water before getting in.

What's this I'm hearing about Harry Potter getting jumped by a gang of youths who pinched his phone and his wallet?
Yes, he was definitely muggied.

I'd tell you the essence of my Sartre joke but I'm not sure if it actually exists.

Gustave Doré's figure of death sitting on a globe from Edgar Allan Poe's 'The Raven' (1883).

I went to the hairdresser today and told him I wanted my hair cut like Truman Capote. So he made me sit on a pile of magazines.

For my nephew's christening present I bought a huge compendium of every story Dahl ever wrote. They're all Roald into one.

I just picked up a voicemail with the sound of seagulls in the background from a guy called Richard. Should I call him Bach?

If William Wordsworth were alive today, what would he be doing?
Trying to get out of his coffin.

Ben Travers walks into a bar holding a huge script. The barman asks: "Why the long farce?"

How does the Pope buy books online?
He uses his PaPal account.

What did the headlouse in Robinson Crusoe's hair say to the other headlouse in Robinson Crusoe's hair? "I'm off now, see you on Friday."

Der neue Robinson auf der einsamen Ratten Insel, im Süd-Meere St. Helena genannt.

Dr Frankenstein: I took the Bride of Frankenstein to the Caribbean last week.
Igor: Jamaica?
Dr Frankenstein: Yes

Satirical print (1815) portraying Napoleon Bonaparte cast away as Daniel Defoe's Robinson Crusoe.

I've just had a new *Lord of the Rings*-themed kitchen installed. The grill and the oven are great but I really like the hob bit.

Who was JRR Tolkien's favourite singer?
Elvish Presley

Why can you never overtake Gandalf in a car?
Because you shall not pass.

How does Gandalf prefer to travel?
Fly, you fools.

Why is it impossible to get into Sauron's sitting room?
Because there's always one Mordor.

Why did Frodo turn his mobile phone off?
He was nervous that the ring would give him away.

I'm a bit doubtful about this new extended version of *The Hobbit*. Bilbo's 6ft tall now.

My English teacher said I had to write 500 words on the new Sally Rooney novel, but during lunchtime I only did about 30 before the school librarian snatched it back off me.

I was amazed on my first day as a warder in the high-security prison to see so many of the inmates reading *Ducks, Newburyport*, but then I realised that they're quite used to long sentences.

I was flicking through my boyfriend's copy of *The Da Vinci Code* and he's written my name on the inside cover. So it looks like I'm in his bad books.

I couldn't work out why the members of my book club were chucking copies of Stephen King's novels all over the place. But then *It* hit me.

I've mislaid my copy of the first book in Michael Grant's series about adults disappearing. It's *Gone*.

Playwright Christopher Marlowe wore pretty chic clothes for the 16th century. He was always dressed to quill.

Frankenstein's monster answers a knock at the door and the postman hands him a large packet addressed to 'Frankenstein'. The monster hands it back. "House opposite," he says, "but don't worry, common mistake."

Why was Dr Frankenstein so muscle-bound?
He was a very keen bodybuilder.

I'd tell you my Marcel Proust joke but I've forgotten how it…
[chomp, chomp], ah, now I remember!

My Mary Shelley joke is so good it'll leave you in stitches.

I'm only going to tell you my Alexandre Dumas joke vingt ans
après.

My great grandfather insists somebody is creeping into his sitting
room at night and stealing his copies of Agatha Christie's books.
I'm worried he's losing his Marples.

Pádraig comes to England and applies for a job on a building site.
To test his knowledge, the foreman asks: "What's the difference
between a joist and a girder?". "Ah, that's an easy one," says
Pádraig. "The first wrote *Ulysses* and the other wrote *Faust.*"

Which witty playwright was scared by Christmas?
Noel Coward

The one piece of advice that Gabriel García Márquez taught me
over dinner was never to be a name-dropper.

I had a really bad day today. I had two volumes of the collected
works of Hegel on the back seat of my car and somebody
smashed the side window and left two more.

Collective nouns

A tenet of palindromes

An obscurity of poets

A pan of literary critics

A deal of literary agents

A block of authors

A Ferrari of royalties

After years on my TBR pile, I have at last read *Endgame*. So I can finally cross it off my Beckett list.

"Your diary is really good," said his wife.
"My thoughts exactly," replied Samuel Pepys.

Last week I tried to make a Faustian pact, but – damn you autocorrect – I ended up making a Proustian one instead, and now I just lie around all day in bed remembering things.

Have you heard about this new book by Amber Greene about traffic lights?
Yep, I've just finished it. I've read Amber Greene.

I just started the last chapter of *A Suitable Boy* when my daughter asked me, "Mum, why is your book so thick?" "Well," I told her, "it's a long story."

Robert Frost: Two roads diverged in a wood, and I – I took the one less traveled by.
Mrs Frost: **Well your tea's cold now.**

What's the difference between *Romeo and Juliet* and COVID-19? **One's a coronavirus and the other's a Verona crisis.**

Did you know that Stephen King's son is called Joseph? **I'm not joking but he is.**

Why does Wally always wear a stripey shirt? **Because he doesn't want to be spotted.**

Dialogues Concerning Natural Religion by David Hume was published in 1779 after his death. To put it another way, it was published posthumeously.

Not many people know that Charles Dickens's A Tale of Two Cities was first published in two local newspapers. It was the Bicester times, it was the Worcester times…

The death of Juliette as illustrated in Émile Montégut's French edition of the *Complete Works of Shakespeare* (1870).

ROMEO & JULIETTE

Did you know that Donald Trump writes all his own books?
Honestly?
Well…

Ladies and gentlemen please put your hands together to welcome Nicci Gerrard and Sean French, two thriller writers who need no introduction. Because they're married.

What do you call a writer who balances pints of lager on their head while playing snooker?
Beatrix Potter.

I dropped into my local bookshop to buy a copy of *1984* but they'd only got *Animal Farm*. I thought, Orwell never mind!

My friend wasn't quite sure if she'd like Jane Austen's books, but I gave her plenty of encouragement and now she loves them. All she needed was a little *Persuasion*.

When F Scott Fitzgerald got a bad cold, he went to bed with a bottle of whisky and within a couple of hours it had gone. Although of course he still had a cold.

Have you forgotten that I lent you my copy of *Normal People?*
Nope, but I'm fairly sure I will soon.

The second person to receive the coronavirus vaccine in England was called William Shakespeare, aged 81, and from Warwickshire. But there's a rumour going round that actually the second person was Christopher Marlowe but Shakespeare took the credit.

Terrible timetable today. All my lectures this morning were on Shakespeare's plays. All the ones this afternoon are on his poetry. It's all going from Bard to Verse.

Shakespeare walks into a bar. "Not you again," says the landlady, "you're bard".

What do you call a man with shrubland habitat and a seagull on his head?
Heathcliff.

Why did Puck cross the road?
Because he saw someone he knew Oberon the other side.

Did you know that Aristophanes once wrote a drama all about puns?
It was a play on words.

If George Eliot were alive today, what would she be famous for?
Being 200 years old.

Why did Graham Greene cover his manuscripts in gold paint?
Because he had a gilt complex.

What do you call a poet with a tortoise on his head?
Shelley.

Why is a schoolgirl on half term like Sir Walter Scott with a little cold?
They both have a week off.

Why have Basset dogs got big ears?
Because Noddy refused to pay the ransom.

Why does George RR Martin wear braces?
To keep his trousers up.

Which writer should you ask for some liquid mercury?
HG Wells.

This first edition of Bambi is quite costly.
Yes, it's a little dear.

The next part of the Frozen movie franchise is a novel by Olaf about his early life. It's a bildungsnowman.

'The painting. It is your best work, Basil, the best thing you have ever done'. Frontispiece to Oscar Wilde's *The Picture of Dorian Gray* (1910).

Even though it was written in 1849, *Civil Disobedience* is so easy to read. I put it down to Thoreau editing.

What kind of cherries did Voltaire prefer?
Candied.

I love telling people spoilers about *The Picture of Dorian Gray*. Never gets old.

Customer: I'm looking for a book about class consciousness and the socialist means of production.
Bookseller: Have you read Marx?
Customer: Well, a few, but the doctor said they should fade soon.

Customer: Do you have the audiobook of *Wolf Hall?*
Bookseller: Yes, here it is.
Customer: Thanks, although I'm really after the large print version because it's for my grandpa and he's quite deaf.

John Milton is a real liability when he's playing Yahtzee. Every time it's his turn, there is a pair of dice lost.

What kind of shoes does Paddington wear?
None. He has bear feet.

What strange literary artefact did they uncover in Uncle Tom's Cabin?
Harriet Beecher's toe.

I fancy a curry tonight – I think I'll go for a Tarka Masala.
Don't you mean a Tikka Masala?
Nope, it's quite similar, but it's just a little 'otter.

- When was Patricia Highsmith's birthday?
- January 19
- Which year?
- Every year

I wasn't feeling well so I went to see my GP yesterday. He asked about my diet and I told him I'd been chomping through the works of Jane Austen. He advised me to go easy on those and get stuck into *Brighton Rock* and *Our Man in Havana* because I wasn't eating nearly enough Greenes.

Customer: I'm looking for a copy of *Possession.*
Bookseller: Byatt?
Customer: Of course. If I wanted to steal it, I'd hardly have told you first.

Customer: Do you have a copy of *Gravity's Rainbow?*
Bookseller: Pynchon?
Customer: Absolutely not, I want to buy it.

Mum, what's your opinion of *The Silmarillion?*
It makes absolutely no sense at all.
I know, but let's hear it anyway.

What's the difference between a fisherman and Franz Kafka?
One baits his hooks and the other hates his books.

Why did Odysseus grab a bar of soap when Poseidon wrecked his ship?
To wash himself ashore.

What is a flea's favourite read?
The Itch Hiker's Guide to the Galaxy.

Why do people sometimes get asthma if they haven't read Charlotte Brontë?

It can be hard to breathe with no Eyre.

Who is Emily Dickinson's favourite Christmas reindeer?

Dasher.

Peter asked me why I'm always curled up at the back of my wardrobe reading a book. I told him it's Narnia business.

Doctor, doctor, I keep dreaming that I'm writing *The Hobbit*.

Don't worry sir, you've just been Tolkien in your sleep.

Charlotte Brontë
portrayed in
an engraving
after George
Richmond's
painting (1857).

I'm normally quite laid back but now it looks like somebody's pinched one of my Mr Men books. No more Mr Nice Guy.

What do you call a Belgian detective with an air conditioning unit on his head?
Air cool.

There was 33% off all book titles at my local bookshop this week, so I bought a copy of *Eats, Shoots.*

Customer: Do you have any books by Shakespeare?
***Bookseller:* We certainly do. Which one?**
Customer: William.

She's an excellent agent. She managed to get the dwarfs from Snow White a seven-figure book deal.

Why are *Wolf Hall* and *Bring up the Bodies* afraid of *The Mirror and the Light?*
Because they know it'll always be after them.

I've just begun a speed-reading course. Last night I read Infinite Jest in 15 seconds. I know it's only two words, but I'm still a beginner.

What does Charles Dickens always keep in his spice rack?
The best of thyme, the worst of thyme.

It was packed at that celebrity author's reading this morning. Suppose it was ok, but it would have been much better if they'd done it out loud.

I deleted all the audiobook fairy tales off of my smartphone. Now it's Hans-free.

And finally, one for Audrey Niffenegger fans…
The barman says: "We don't serve time travellers in here."
A man walks into the bar.

'The Sea Rises' by Phiz as featured in Dickens's *A Tale of Two Cities* (1859).

THE SEA RISES.

04

Book Jokes
in Films

In Die Another Day (2002), James Bond (Pierce Brosnan)
looks at a book called *Birds of the West Indies*, written by the
ornithologist James Bond, Ian Fleming's inspiration for his secret
agent. Bond also describes himself as an ornithologist when he
meets Jinx, played by Halle Berry.

Central to the James Bond film Spectre (directed by Sam
Mendes, who studied English at the University of Cambridge)
is the theme of memory. So it's interesting that French actress
Léa Seydoux plays a character called Madeleine Swann, a nod
to the remembrance properties of the famous shell-like sponge
cake in literary history in Marcel Proust's opening volume *Du
côté de chez Swann* in his novel series *À la recherche du temps
perdu*.

Mendes also directed Skyfall which some critics have likened to
Sir Thomas Malory's *Le Morte d'Arthur*, especially the pre-title
sequence (betrayal by a woman, 'dies' in a lake, 'reborn' when
England is in peril) with Q as Merlin providing a new sword in
the stone (a gun that only Bond's palmprint can operate), and
the new M called Gareth Mallory. Judi Dench's character M also

recites lines from Tennyson's poetry cycle *Idylls of the King*, a retelling of the Arthurian legend.

At the end of Notting Hill (1999) directed by Roger Mitchell, Hugh Grant's character William Thacker is seen clearly reading *Captain Corelli's Mandolin* by Louis de Bernières. Mitchell was due to direct the film version of the novel next (but sadly had to pull out after suffering a heart attack). Similarly, in When Harry Met Sally (1989), Harry (Billy Crystal) is seen reading *Misery* by Stephen King in bed. Reiner's next project was the film of the book.

In Jurassic Park, a shot of its merchandise offerings includes the real-life book *The Making of Jurassic Park* by Don Shay and Jody Duncan. Later in the film, Tim (Joseph Mazzello) – the nephew of the park's owner John Hammond – meets paleontologist Dr Alan Grant (Sam Neill). Tim is carrying Grant's book called *Dinosaur Detectives* which claims to include a foreword by Sir Richard Attenborough, who plays Hammond.

'I'm a writer, but then nobody's perfect'.
Billy Wilder's tombstone

* In the film adaptation of *Strangers On A Train* (1951) directed by Alfred Hitchcock, Farley Granger (played by Guy Haines) is seen reading *Alfred Hitchcock's Fireside Book of Suspense* (1947).

* In Looking for Mr. Goodbar (1977), Diane Keaton is sitting at a bar and reading *The Godfather*, in which she starred in 1972.

* In the 2014 film Interstellar, many of the titles on the bookcase – which plays a key part in the plot – include themes directly related to the action, including *Flatland* by Edwin Abbott which focues on the existence of multiple dimensions, and *A Wrinkle in Time* by Madeleine L'Engle which is all about space, time, and tesseracts …

And finally, here's a tweet by Chris Addison on October 30, 2020:

* "For The Hustle, which I directed exactly three years ago, we had Anne Hathaway's character read the French translation of *The Curious Incident of The Dog In The Night-Time* because the lead fella, Alex Sharp, had won a Tony for his performance in the play."

05

Books &
Bookcases

Sometimes when I get angry I knock over a chair or two, but I'd never do that to my bookcase. I have too much shelf-respect.

You've got too many books!
No, I haven't got enough bookshelves.

I ripped off my fingernail while I was tightening up my Billy bookcase today. Very much a shelf-inflicted injury.

What's the best system for book-keeping?
Never lend them.

I can't stop buying bookcases. I've just got no shelf-control.

Why is it such a pain hanging out with books?
They don't have any shelf-awareness.

What happens if you get caught gluing the pages of a biography together?
Multiple back-to-back life sentences.

Why are hardbacks so brave?
They have strong spines.

How does a book keep warm in the winter?
It puts on a book jacket.

TURRIS BABEL

'The Tower
of Babel' by
Athanasius
Kircher (1679)

06

Bookshops

My friend is a novelist and the other day he went into a bookshop and got really angry with the manager because no copies of his books were going through the tills. It seems his story didn't check out.

This new book about poltergeists is flying off the shelves.

A man goes into a bookshop run by a dishonest antiquarian bookseller and shows him a picture on his phone of a signed Shakespeare First Folio.
"I found this old book in the attic," he says, **"and wondered if it's worth anything?"**
"Afraid not," says the book dealer, "but I'm running out of paper to line my parrots' birdcages, so if I can come to your house later this afternoon and pick it up, I can give you a tenner for it."
When he arrives, the man hands him a box of shredded paper.
"What's this?" says the bookseller
"It's the book. I felt bad about charging you a tenner for it so I thought I'd do you a favour and rip it all up for you."

The title-page of the First Folio which bears Martin Droeshout's celebrated portrait of William Shakespeare (1623).

Mr. WILLIAM
SHAKESPEARES

COMEDIES,
HISTORIES, &
TRAGEDIES.

Published according to the True Originall Copies.

Martin Droeshout sculpsit London.

LONDON
Printed by Isaac Iaggard, and Ed. Blount. 1623.

Why are bookshop employees so law-abiding?
They do everything by the book.

So I nipped into my local bookshop to have a look at their books about conspiracies, but there wasn't a single copy. Coincidence?

Customer: Could I have a book for my son please?
***Bookseller:* I'm afraid we don't do swaps.**

Bookseller: Can I help you?
***Customer:* Well actually I'm after quite a lot of different books.**
Bookseller: Not a problem. Do you have a list?
***Customer:* No, I always stand like this.**

Customer to second-hand bookseller: Would you take anything off for cash?
***Second-hand bookseller:* No. This is a bookshop, not a strip club.**

The bookshop's new assistant is up in court today. He was caught with his hand in the tale.

Customer: Excuse me, where is the section on pantomimes please?
***Bookseller:* It's behind you!**
Customer: OH no it isn't!
***Bookseller:* OH yes it is!**

A policeman was on his regular foot beat when he saw a woman coming towards him walking a giraffe.

"You ought to take that animal to the zoo," he said.

The next day, he saw the same woman with the same giraffe again.

"I thought I told you to take him to the zoo," said the policeman.

"I did," said the woman, "and today I'm taking him to the bookshop."

"Excuse me, I'm looking for that new book about turtles."

"Hardback?"

"Absolutely. And with little heads."

I had an excellent day today. There was a big display of that new bestseller in the bookshop window, *How to Solve 50% of Your Problems*. So I bought two.

What is Donald Trump's favourite bookshop?
Borders.

Customer: Have you got that new book about groundhogs?
Bookseller: **I'm afraid it hasn't come out yet.**

Customer: I'm looking for a book about Erwin Schrödinger and Ivan Pavlov.
Bookseller: **Now, that does ring a bell but I'm not sure if it's in the stockroom or not.**

What did the bookseller say when she found a root vegetable on the shelves?
Blimey, that's a turnip for the books.

My local bookshop has gone into partnership with the clothes store next door and now they're both full of text aisles.

Never judge a book by its coverage.

07

Cookbooks

Have you been eating bread sticks over this joke book?
Yes, but how can you tell?
All the jokes are a bit crumby.

KFC has just released its new winter catalogue of zesty cookbooks. It's a mixture of eleven blurbs and spices.

Why was the chef upset to find somebody had ripped the recipe for chili salsa out of his new cookbook?
It was his chief sauce of income.

There's a new addition to the Fifty Shades franchise, a cookbook called *Fifty Shades of Gravy*. I hear it's extremely saucy.

Why are science fiction novels like cookbooks?
You keep thinking, 'well, that's never going to happen'.

Why did the accountant's fastfood restaurant go bust?
He refused to cook the books.

TINNED PROVISIONS, INCLUDING FISH, MEAT, GAME, FRUIT AND
HOUSEHOLD REQUISITES.

This soup book is very hard to track down in bookshops. It's always out of stock.

My new book is called *101 Different Ways to Chop Onions*. Read it and weep.

Louise Glück, Patrick Modiano and Kazuo Ishiguro go into a pub and order three pints of beer.
"That'll be £27 please," says the barman. "You know," he says proudly, "we don't get many winners of the Nobel prize for literature in here."
"At £9 a pint I'm not surprised," says Ishiguro.

I'm tempted to tell you my latest cookbook joke, but I'm rising above it.

What's yellow, smells of almonds, and swings through the jungle?
Tarzipan.

Why do so many bakers write cookbooks?
Because they knead the dough.

What is a butcher's favourite literary device?
A meataphor.

Why was the food critic fired?
They didn't reference their sauces.

Illustration from Mrs Beeton's *The Book of Household Management* (1892 edition).

08

Fake Books

When private libraries began to become more public from
the 18th century onwards, their owners also began having fun
by filling some of the shelves with fake or 'sham' books, often
made of wood. These spines sported humorous titles, some
admittedly funnier than others. Belton House has one of the
earliest selections dating back to the 1740s, including titles such
as *Paradise Improv'd* and *Wooden Lectures*, while the window
shutters at the National Trust's Mount Stewart property in
Northern Ireland are covered in spines with titles of lost/
imaginary works. These rather intellectual in-jokes include the
now vanished *Nine Comedies* by Edmund Spenser, and 'works' by
ancient female Greek philospher Hipparchia of Maroneia, none
of whose writings survive.

At some point in the 1820s, Sir Thomas Dyke Acland had the
following attached to a door in the library at his home, Killerton
House in Devon, also now owned by the National Trust:
* *Complete Art of Lying*
* *Nettles for Nice*
* *Noses Hobble on Corns Wig Without Brains*
* *Hinge's Orations*
* *Squeak on Openings*
* *Bang on Shutting*
The final three are all next to the door's hinges…

The poet and keen punner Thomas Hood provided dozens of
examples for the Duke of Devonshire's library at Chatsworth in
1831 including:
* Shelley's *Conchologist*
* *Pygmalion* by Lord Bacon
* *Percy Vere. In 40 volumes*
* *Cursory Remarks on Swearing*
* *The Scottish Boccaccio* by D. Cameron
* Johnson's *Contradictionary*
* John Knox, *On Death's Door*
* Inigo, *On Secret Entrances*
* Captain Parry, *Designs for Friezes* [Parry was a famous Arctic
explorer of the period]

Charles Dickens commissioned an entire fake bookcase for his
London home at Tavistock Place in 1851. Among the spines he
invented were:
* *Jonah's Account of the Whale*
* *Steele.* By the Author of "Ion"
* *Lady Godiva on the Horse*
* *Hansard's Guide to Refreshing Sleep*

When he moved house to Gad's Hill in Kent, he had another
made, a disguised bookcase door for his study, including:
* Malthus's *Nursery Songs*
* *Swallows on Emigration*
* *Shelley's Oysters*
* *Noah's Arkitecture*
* *Mag's Diversions* [an early working title for *David Copperfield*]
* *Cats' Lives* (nine volumes)

The fake bookcase/door in the library at Oxburgh Hall, Norfolk, another National Trust property, even includes a fake book called 'La Porte'…

The Chatsworth collection was updated in the 1960s by travel writer Patrick Leigh Fermor. His offerings included:
* *Shadow Cabinets* by A. Ghost Writer
* *Reduced to the Ranks* by D. Motion,
* *Gloucester in All Weathers* by Dr Foster
* *Consenting Adults* by Abel N. Willing
* *Dipsomania* by Mustafa Swig
* *The Battle of the Bulge* by Lord Slim

And rather cheekily:
Book Titles by Patrick Leigh Fermor

More recently, the Charities Advisory Trust launched a Christmas card through its Card Aid initiative featuring spines of such must-read books as:
* *The Reindeer Elk & Caribou Handbook* published by Prancer & Vixen
* *Know Your Snow* by Crispen Evans
* *Whose Flue: A complete guide to chimney identification* by Sue T Smutts
* *Gathering Winter Fuel: Your Legal Position*
* *Jingle Bells & Tinnitus – A Study* by Dr. AL DeWay
* *Thermal Underwear for the Fuller Figure – A Guide*
* *Where Everyone Lives* vol XII
* *The Big Book of Good and Bad Boys and Girls* Vol I

Foreign Language

If you have your nose stuck in a book you are a 'bookworm' in English and a...

Library mouse in Portuguese

Book flea in Indonesian

Reading horse in Icelandic

Book insect in Japanese

Read rat in German

Ink drinker in French

Reading maggot in Finnish

Book moth in Czech

I like to read books in translation.
My favourite is *Celsius 232.778*.

Egal wie dicht du bist, Goethe war Dichter.

Pourquoi Flaubert n'était jamais sûr de la qualité de son travail? **Parce que le beau varie.**

This morning I forgot the French word for strawberry, so I had to look it up in a fraise book.

I really love the complexity of Chinese fiction. For a start, there are so many characters.

Guest list at the book prizegiving party

Mr & Mrs Katbedtime, and their son, Boo

Mr & Mrs Dinglybrarey, and their son, Len

Mr & Mrs Sellers, and their daughter, Bess

Mr & Mrs Scabin, and their uncle Tom

Mr and Mrs Anory, and their son Jack

Mr & Mrs Teesfolcon, and their daughter, Moll

Mr & Mrs Toositties, and their son, Attila

Mr & Mrs Malfarm, and their daughter, Annie

Mr & Mrs Tenspage, and their son, Con

Mr & Mrs Miserables, and their son, Les.

Mr & Mrs Fertbükfayre, and their son, Frank

10

Grammar

Grammarians constantly like to make fun of gerunds. They're a running joke.

Q: Can you run through a scout campsite?
A: No, you can only 'ran' because it's past tents.

At my job interview, I was told that my boss was a stickler for punctuation so naturally I made sure that I was bang on time for my first day at work.

Which word becomes shorter after you add two letters to it?
Short.

How do you console a grammar Nazi?
"There, their, they're."

Why did the comma stop dating the apostrophe?
Because it was always so possessive.

Q: What happened when the verb asked the noun to conjugate?
A: The noun declined.

A bar was walked into by the passive voice.

Two speech marks walk into a "bar".

A synonym saunters into an inn.

At close of play, a cliché walks into a bar, happy as Larry, good to go, and smart as a whip.

Grammarland book for children by ML Nesbitt (1889).

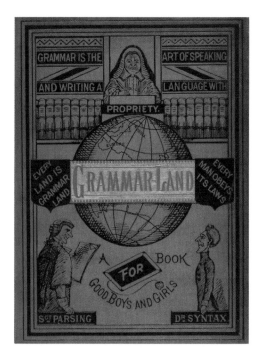

11

Graphics

Old cartoonists never die, they just go into suspended animation.

I'm going to marry a pencil and I'm looking forward to introducing my parents to my bride, 2B.

Highlighter pens are the future. Mark my words.

My friend Emma works in her garden office illustrating books, but it's a bit dark because she always draws the curtains.

Remember that the word stifle is an anagram of itself.

There's hardly been any news about that graphic novelist who died yesterday. Details are sketchy.

Of course this book of sketches by war artists is huge, they kept drawing enemy fire.

This series of books on graffiti art has been getting worse and worse with each edition. I'm afraid the writing's been on the wall for a while.

Crossword compiler: I've been racking my brains for a word for two weeks.
Production editor: You mean a fortnight?

What happens when a team of graphic novelists plays football against a team of comic illustrators?
It always finishes in a draw.

For years I've got on really well with the guy who illustrates all my books, and then yesterday out of the blue he drew a knife on me. It took ages to get the felt tip off.

All the comic books my older sister gave me had their final pages ripped out. I had to draw my own conclusions.

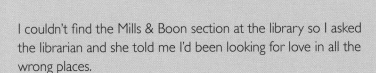

12

Libraries

I couldn't find the Mills & Boon section at the library so I asked the librarian and she told me I'd been looking for love in all the wrong places.

After long consideration, I've resigned from my job in the library. I think it was about time. Maybe even overdue.

What are all those piranhas doing rushing about in the library? **They're in a reading frenzy.**

Man in library: "Have you got any book on cliffhangers?"
Librarian:

Everybody who got a new book from me as a Christmas present this year, a quick reminder that they are due back at the library before February.

Man walks into a library and says: "I hope you don't have a book on reverse psychology."

B. Picart del. et Sculp. dir. 1726.

Taking a page out of someone's book isn't always a good strategy. It got me thrown out of the library.

My friend went into our local library and asked if they had any books on the *Titanic*. "Absolutely, dozens and dozens," replied the librarian. "That's a shame," he said. "They must all be ruined by now."

It took me a while to track down that novel about religious women. The library had put it in the nun-fiction section.

An *Oxford English Dictionary* and a *Roget's Thesaurus* are in a school library when the school caretaker puts them in a box for recycling. "I can see you're very distressed about this," the thesaurus says to the dictionary. "You don't even know the meaning of the word," replies the dictionary. "But I know what it's like," says the thesaurus.

Why did you get kicked out of the library for miming to your friend?
The librarian told me that actions speak louder than words.

A woman approaches the information desk in the library and asks the librarian: "Excuse me, do you have a bookmark?" The librarian replies: "Yes, I've got a box of them here, but my name's Tony."

A woman reading in a library from *Biblothèque des Dames* (Amsterdam, 1716).

Why do so many Americans keep guns in their home libraries?
It's for shelf-defence.

I went to the library to get a book on abdominal pain but it was missing a whole section. Somebody had ripped the appendix out.

What's the first thing a librarian puts up in her new baby's bedroom?
A bookmobile.

If I'm in the mood for reading some fiction, I head to the library. If I've got a fancy for some non-fiction, I go to the truthbrary.

I spent years working as an accountant, so when I wanted to retrain I decided to become a librarian because I'm such a good book-keeper.

What is the poshest building?
The library, because all the books have titles.

I've got a good library joke for you, but I'm afraid it's non-circulating.

Librarians always look forward to retiring because then they can enjoy a new chapter in their life.

Man in library: Do you have any books on badgers?
Librarian: No, they'd fall off.

Man: And do you have any on radiators?
Librarian: No, just the normal shelves.

I think they're building a new library in town but nobody seems to know anything about it. It's all very hush-hush.

Why are library carts so rebellious?
It's just how they roll.

When I'm feeling a bit under the weather, I head to a library because they're excellent for circulation.

During my author reading at the local library I kept dropping my book. In the end, they had to ask me to leave because I couldn't control my volume.

There's a court report in today's newspaper about the librarian who was sentenced to life in prison. It seems that the judge threw the book at him.

What do you do if an attractive librarian rolls their eyes at you?
Roll them back.

Overpage:
Specimen room and library from Ferrante Imperato's *Natural History of Minerals, Precious Stones, and Other Curiosities* (Venice, 1672).

RITRATTO
FERRANT

MVSEO DI
PERATO

Literary Shopping

Lord of the Fries (*vegetarian fast food chain in Australia*)

Sweet Expectations (*sweet shop in Rochester, Charles Dickens's home town*)

The Merchant of Tennis (*tennis shop in Toronto*)

Grate Expectations (*fireplace shop in London*)

Cash 22 (*pawnbroker chain in London*)

Tequila Mockingbird (*cocktail bar chain in London*)

Why didn't the burglar break into David Foster Wallace's house?
He was scared he might get a long sentence.

What did the librarian say to the man who took out a 1,000 page book on bodybuilding?
"Don't overdue it."

I searched the library for a guide about how to mend an automatic gearbox, but it seems they only have manuals.

I slipped over again in the library today. That's the last time I browse in the non-friction section.

Man walks into the library. "Have you got any books about paranoia?"
She frowns and whispers: "That's what they WANT you to read."

Improving social mobility in the bookmark community is a challenging project because they always know their place.

Man: CAN I HAVE A SKINNY LATTE AND A BROWNIE PLEASE?
Librarian: **This is a library!**
Man: (whispering) Sorry, can I have a skinny latte and a brownie please?

13

Light Bulbs

How many Dylan Thomases does it take to change a bulb?
None. They just rage, rage against the dying of the light.

How many self-publishers does it take to change a light bulb?
The light bulb shouldn't have to change, it's just stuck-in-a-rut thinking that demands a middleman to effect a transformation.

How many rare book dealers does it take to change a light bulb?
One, but then you can't turn it on as it has to stay in mint condition.

How many typesetters does it take to change a light bulb?
One, but they have to know exactly how tight it should be.

How many vanity publishers does it take to change a light bulb?
As many as you can afford.

How many book editors does it take to change a light bulb?
One, but they want to keep changing it.

How many self-help writers does it take to change a light bulb?
None. It can change itself with some proactive mentoring and calm me-space.

How many children's writers does it take to change a light bulb?
(haughtily) Why are you asking me? **I'm** a literary novelist.

How many writers does it take to change a light bulb?
You want to change the light bulb? I don't THINK so. That's the best part of the whole fitting. I'M NOT CHANGING ANYTHING.

How many proofreaders does it take to change a light bulb?
Proofreaders can't really change light bulbs, they can only query them.

How many book reviewers does it take to change a light bulb?
The problem is they don't know how to do it, but if you have a go they'll be happy to stay comfortably in their chairs and tell you exactly what you're doing wrong.

How many librarians does it take to screw in a light bulb?
645.5

How many copy editors does it take to change a light bulb?
You asked me this in the second draft, and then it seemed to be about fact checkers. Did you mean fact checkers, or should it be altered? See notes below.

Published by William Miller, Albemarle Street, Jan.y 1.1805.

N.º 29.

How many cover blurb writers does it take to screw in a light bulb?

A groundbreaking number… the finest talents to emerge in many years.

How many mystery writers does it take to change a light bulb?

Two. One to screw it almost all the way in, and the other to give it an incredible twist at the end.

How many book commissioning editors does it take to change a light bulb?

Only one, but does it really have to be a light bulb?

Changing a street bulb from William Henry Pyne's *The Costume of Great Britain* (1808).

By the way, I just finished a short book about Edison and the light bulb. It was a bit of light reading.

"Some old lady said that my book left a bad taste in her mouth. I wrote back to her and said, 'You weren't supposed to eat it.'"

Flannery O'Connor

14
Plays

I went to see Lorca's *Blood Wedding* at the theatre last week. Oddly, there was a short break about halfway through the play that we didn't know was planned. Nobody expects the Spanish intermission.

My uncle always argued that the key to successful theatre was to always leave them wanting more. Nice chap, awful anaesthetist.

First theatre-goer: Why are you putting your coat on? It's only the interval.
Second theatre-goer: **Because it says on the programme 'Act 2 – one month later'.**

Did you hear about the scriptwriter on the new remake of Lassie?
He wrote a big part in it for himself. Yep, he gave himself the lead.

F. Hayman Inv.

H. Gravelot sculp.

OTHELLO. Act 4. Sc. 6.

What do cows shout if they don't like a play?
Moo!

The middle-aged actor turned up for the first rehearsal of his new play and found the workshop team building a set that was all made out of purple moss hanging from stuffed elephants perched on a desert island with an upside-down jacuzzi in the middle. "I knew it," said the actor wistfully, "I'm at a strange stage in my life."

The lazy set designer went quietly when the theatre manager sacked him. He didn't make a scene.

Did you hear about the thief who sneaked into the theatre on opening night?
He stole the spotlight.

The stage manager has done a great job this season.
Props to him.

To make it clear where the Montagu family live and where the Capulet family live, the set designer has put a couple of signs above their doorways: a plaque on both their houses.

I'm halfway through writing a script about Samuel Johnson's dictionary for my am-dram group. It's a play on words.

My actor friends who live in a house down the road are delighted with the plush theatre seats they're fitting in their house, but personally I think it's going to end in tiers.

The lead actor in our play is always disappearing through the trap door. It's a stage he's going through.

My friend is planning to set up a new shadow puppet theatre. I've seen his business plan and he could be a millionaire by Christmas, although they are just projected figures.

Acknowledgements

To my daughter Leonora without whose never-failing sympathy and encouragement this book would have been finished in half the time. **The Heart of a Goof** by PG Wodehouse

For Mom (just skip over the sex scenes, please). **No Way Back** by Matthew Klein

To my wife Karen, who is 90% inspiration and 90% patience. No, it doesn't add up to 180%. She multitasks. **I wonder what I'm thinking about** by Moose Allain

15

Poetry

My wife is a percussionist but she's also writing a book of poetry. She uses a lot of cymbalism in her work.

A foot walks into a bar. "Are you a foot?" asks the landlady. The foot replies: "Yes, iamb."

I think the metre on his poem is wrong. It just doesn't ode up.

Did you hear about the useless poet who really dislikes his mother-in-law?
He can't stanza.

My granddaughter always has her nose in a book of Roman poetry. She's an Ovid reader.

I'd tell you my poet joke/but I'm not sure/where to put the/line breaks.

I've got a poetry joke but people keep asking me what it means.

I'd tell you my experimental poetry joke but it's oblong cherry earwax deep down in the ocean.

I'd send you my poetry joke but while you'd thank me for the chance to read it, it's not quite for you, but might work for somebody else.

What has iambic pentameter and fifteen lines?
A baker's sonnet.

I'm thinking of swapping from my course on 17th-century poetry to one about orientalism and postcolonial studies because it's easier Said than Donne.

Why do poets always dip their work in hand moisturiser?
Because everybody enjoys poetry in lotion.

What do you call the judge for a poetry prize?
A poetic justice.

Doctor, doctor, I'm think I've got a dose of fairy stories.
I see, and when did you start having symptoms?
Well, once upon a time.

If you carry a book of poetry then a tiger won't hurt you. As long as you carry it quite fast.

Did you hear about the dipsomaniac lyricist?
He has trouble writing songs because he can't get past the first four bars.

How does a backwards poet write?
Inverse.

Why are milkmaids so good at writing poetry?
The moos is always with them.

Why did Robert Browning write to his future wife Elizabeth after he'd read her poems?
Because he wanted to meter in real life.

Why is a book of poetry like David Icke's theory that lizardlike aliens are running the world?
Nobody buys either one of them.

Why did Philip Larkin always check his wallet before he set off in his car?
He didn't want to get fined for driving without a poetic license.

A scene on the mythical island of Cythère from Paul Verlaine's *Fêtes Galantes* collection of poetry (Paris, 1928).

Why did John Keats hate doing his tax returns?
Because he ode so much.

Geoff had fallen in love with two women, one was a poet, the other owned a fish and chip shop, but he wasn't sure which one to ask to be his wife, to marry for batter or verse.

A group of medical students are being shown around a hospital ward by a doctor.

"And how are you today?" the doctor asks the first patient.

"O, wad some Power the giftie gie us To see oursels as others see us!" she replies.

The doctor asks the elderly gentleman in the next bed the same question.

"There's nought but care on ev'ry han', In every hour that passes, O," he says.

Finally, the doctor asks a young woman in the corner bed how she's feeling.

"Should auld acquaintance be forgot, And never brought to min'? she replies.

One of the students turns to the doctor and says: "What ward are these people on?"

"Ah" says the doctor, "it's the Serious Burns Unit."

Man on first date: "Every time you smile at me it lights up my life."

***Woman:* "That's so lovely. You must be a poet."**

Man: "No, I'm a dentist."

His new book of poetry is like a bath. It's ok when you dip in at the start, but after a while it leaves you cold.

16

Publishers, Agents, & Critics

Last week I sent a proposal to my publisher about a story that took place entirely during a hockey match, but I've just received a rejection letter in the post today. They said they didn't like my pitch.

The publisher has really gone to town on the cover design of this new politics book. Yes, it's a spine of the times.

Agent: My client is thinking of writing an origin story.
Publisher: Not a problem, we're proud to be a prequel opportunities employer.

The publishers have been forced to withdraw their new book about the history of the Black Death. The author is suspected of plaguerism.

Did you hear about the book editor who left his work on the kitchen counter and his wife accidentally turned it into a dessert?
That's hard to believe.
I know, but the proof was in the pudding.

The first known depiction of a printing house and bookshop from Mathias Huss's *Dance of Death* (Lyon, 1499).

I submitted my manuscript for a history of sweets to an agent, but he said I couldn't write for toffee.

I have an agent joke but only 15% of you will get it.

I wrote my autobiography and sent it off to dozens of publishers. They all turned it down. Story of my life.

Is a book on voyeurism a peeping tome?

Just got my royalty payment from my publisher today.
Feels more like a peasantry one.

My friend wrote a novel last year and just let me know he's
finally got an agent. I told him how happy my relationship with
my agent has made me. But he's still going to sign up with him
anyway.

Publisher: You got nearly £100 in royalties this month.
Writer: Only £99 this time?
Publisher: No, £00.

Publishers only seem interested in extremist stories. They see
everything in black and white.

My publisher asked me to ghostwrite a cookbook for an award-
winning curry restaurant. It's so secret they're insisting that I sign
a naan-disclosure agreement.

Why aren't you playing tennis with your agent anymore?
**Well, would you play with a man who cheats on line calls,
steals balls from players on neighbouring courts, and always
turns up late for games?**
No, I definitely wouldn't.
Nor will my agent.

I've had a good relationship with my agent for ten years. I reckon
ten out of thirty is quite good.

Normally, my publisher insists that the printers only use ink
made in England for my books. But they want to surprise
everybody with my next novel and get it from a manufacturer in
Madrid because nobody expects the Spanish ink edition.

A book review only really requires a second glance.

Why is working in publishing like being the parent of a toddler?
You have to read the same book over and over again.

What's the difference between publishers and terrorists?
You can negotiate with terrorists.

When I finished my book I took it down south to a publisher in
London. "Is it a tome?" they asked. "Course not, yer daft apeth," I
said, "it's here in t'bag."

Rare Books

I've looked in all the medical books and all over the internet but I can't work out why I've got these light brown spots all over my body. I'm slightly foxed.

I'd tell you my rare books joke, and while at first you'll probably think it's exactly the same as all the other rare books jokes, it has unique provenance and features.

This 18th-century volume about the history of music is very rare but also highly collectible. I think it's a sound investment.

I made a deal last week for two rare volumes of Piranesi etchings which have just fallen to pieces. I hope it's not binding.

That joke about the dusty secondhand book rings a bell. It's already been used.

I heard a joke about trials and tribulations of rare book dealers the other day. It was a fine one.

Reading

How do you start a speedreading competition?
On your bookmark, get set, go!

My teenage son always starts getting moody when he gets about halfway through a new book. I guess he's just at an awkward page.

I was driving down the M1 motorway yesterday and saw a man in the outside lane reading a novel while he was overtaking. I was so angry that I stopped texting and gave him a beep.

After three years I finally finished my first novel. I enjoyed it so much I might read another one.

I'm thinking of buying a book on phobias but I'm a bit scared it won't help me.

Bibliotherapy. Now that's a novel prescription.

I'm a bit disappointed with my new book, *Murder on the Golf Course*. The plot is full of holes.

This book about how the author got abducted by aliens is far too long. I think he just got carried away.

Why are high-rise car parks a good place to look for books?
Because they're multi-storied.

Just finished reading a book about the effects of light pollution on the night sky. Two stars.

I've finally got to that juicy thriller at the bottom of my TBR pile. ISBN waiting for you...

Tinder bio: I like my men how I like my books, well-read and leather-bound.

It took me ages to get started on this book about the history of Sellotape. I just couldn't find the beginning.

Have you ever tried reading a book upside down?
I found it tricky trying to keep my legs up in the air.

DUMMHEIT

MISANTROPIE

PRUEDERIE

FRÖMMELEI

Have you read that new novel about a malevolent tornado?
There's a real twist at the end.

So what book are you reading now?
Ah, well, it's a bit of a mystery.
But doesn't it say on the cover?

He's not a big reader but he is extremely organised. He's
only got one book in his library at home but it's ALWAYS in
alphabetical order.

I don't have the patience to read a whole book series, so now
I've finished my history of World War I, I'm going to skip the
next nine volumes and go straight to one about World War II.

Back when I was young, all fairy stories used to start 'Once upon
a time', but now they begin 'If I'm elected I promise…'

What do you call a bookworm who can't stop reading about
strong female characters?
A heroine addict!

The dangers of reading
– stupidity, misanthropy,
prudery and bigotry – as
suggested in the German
satirical magazine
Simplicissimus (1896).

I just read an incredible book about mazes.
I got totally lost in it.

Why are the venues at the Hay Festival so fresh?
Because they're full of fans.

Why did the archaeologist's autobiography sell so poorly?
Because her career was in ruins.

My thoughtful partner bought me a book for Christmas called *How to Hug*. Now I just need the other 51 volumes of the encyclopedia for the complete set.

A colonoscopy is a lot like reading a book. As soon as you get to the appendix, it's all over.

My teenage grandson asked me to make him a bookshelf but now he just moans that the books are hurting his back.

Why was the short story so popular on Tinder?
He had a good opening line.

How do you track a book?
Follow its footnotes.

Why does a panther use his tail as a bookmark?
So he doesn't lose his place when he stops reading.

More satire as
Simplicissimus
delivers the tale
of 'The Forbidden
Book' (1896).

Das verbotene Buch

(Von F. Reznicek)

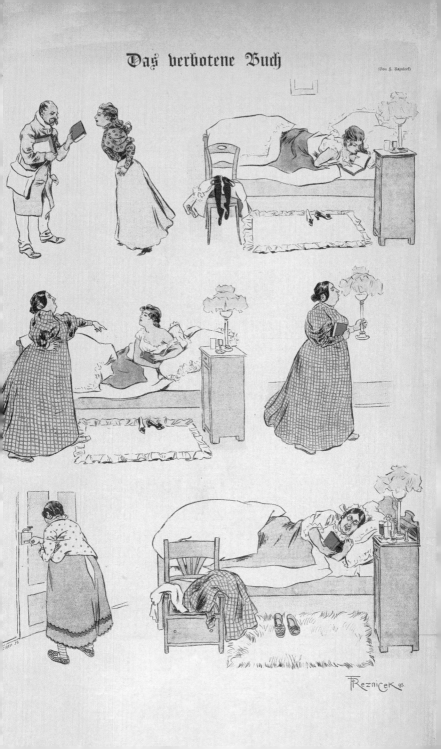

My friend got a poetry book stuck in his mouth but luckily I managed to winkle it out. "Glad to be able to breathe again, I bet" I said to him. "You took the words right out of my mouth," he replied.

I'm halfway through a book about a Victorian psychic.
What's it like?
Medium.

This book about black holes really draws you in.

What is Jeremy Clarkson's favourite book genre?
Autobiography.

My enormous plate of spaghetti got into the *Guinness Book of Records*. I'm having a devil of a job cleaning it off.

Who are the quickest readers?
Demolition experts. They can go through loads of stories in just a few minutes.

I've just read a book all about Stockholm Syndrome. It wasn't much fun at the beginning, but by the time I got to the end I thought it was amazing.

What do you get if you cross a writer with a deadline?
A really clean house.

Did you hear about the scientist who was reading a book about helium?
He couldn't put it down.

Two explorers were in a clearing in the jungle. One was studying a book, the other was scribbling in his notepad when suddenly a tiger leapt out of the trees. He took a quick look at them both and then ate the man reading the book because he knew that readers digest and writers cramp.

Why did the ghost always need more books?
She went through them too fast.

I never go anywhere without my books of maps. I would be lost without them.

How often do you read magazines?
Periodically.

19

Reference Books

I got so bored during lockdown that I started reading my dictionary straight through from the start. I'm now past caring.

Did I tell you about my near-death experience?
I looked up 'dearth' in the dictionary.

When push comes to shove, I'll buy a thesaurus.

The first rule of Write Club is that you do not chit-chat, gossip, discuss, mention, or allude to Write Club.
No, that's Thesaurus Club.

I'm starting as a junior reviser for the new *Oxford English Dictionary* tomorrow so I rang them this morning to check that I'd be starting at nine. "Absolutely not," said my boss, "you'll be starting at Aardvark."

Breaking News: The writer of what one reviewer has slammed as the worst thesaurus ever written has rebutted the accusation saying the criticism is wrong, wrong, and wrong.

I thought there were too many authors to cite, but actually it was no problem *et al.*

I got a brand new thesaurus for Christmas but actually it's nothing to write house about.

My son has had his thesaurus stolen. Now he's lost for words.

This book of London maps is useless. It tells you how to get from A to B but that's no good to me because I live in Q.

I asked my son to get me a phone book. He raised his eyebrows and said: "You're such a dinosaur, just use my phone." So I walloped it against the wall to kill the spider.

I've taken the plunge and decided to upgrade my dictionary to high-definition.

What happens if you gargle with a book of synonyms?
It gives you a really thesaurus throat.

How do you pronounce 'VOLIX'?
Volume nine

He's a few chapters short of a novel.

It took him ages to look up 'vegetarian' in the dictionary until he realised it was in alphabetical order.

Irate man in library: "This is a terrible book. It's got a meaningless plot and I couldn't keep track of the hundreds of characters."
***Librarian:* "Well, that is the phone book, sir."**

The police raided my house early this morning and took way my textbooks on number theory, non-Euclidean geometry, and differential equations. They said I was stockpiling weapons of math instruction.

"You know things are messed up when librarians start marching".

Sign at Occupy Wall Street 2011.

20

Rejections

Deluged by manuscripts, publishers send out many, many rejection letters, but time and hindsight offer the reassurance that the joke is often on them:

It's a great story but sadly also an urban legend that Herman Melville was turned down by publishers Bentley & Son with the line: "First, we must ask, does it have to be a whale?" Nor is it true that Margaret Mitchell's *Gone With the Wind* was rejected 38 times. Or indeed even once.

However, while admitting that it is "a distinguished piece of writing… very skilfully handled", TS Eliot did put it to George Orwell that *Animal Farm* was probably too much political dynamite for Faber to publish. He also made the intriguing plot criticism that it was a good thing that intelligent porkers were in charge of the farm and that "what was needed, (someone might argue), was not more communism but more public-spirited pigs."

Many other writers can also look back in laughter. "Stick to your teaching, Miss Alcott," publisher James Fields rather pompously advised the author of *Little Women*. "You can't write."

Meanwhile, *The Wind in the Willows* by Kenneth Grahame was turned down on the basis that it was "an irresponsible holiday story that will never sell".

Of course there are rejections and rejections, some – though still likely to make the decisionmaker wince in retrospect – letting down the writer more gently than others. William Golding's *Lord of the Flies* was given the thumbs down by Cape who said that: "It does not seem to us that you have been wholly successful in working out an admittedly promising idea", but then sugar-coating the rejection by suggesting that Golding send it to another publisher, André Deutsch, instead.

Nor are literary agents exempt. "The first agent I ever queried sent back a slip saying 'My list is full. The folder you sent wouldn't fit in the envelope'," tweeted JK Rowling in 2015 in response to a query about waiting nervously from potential agents. She later joked: "I now have over a million folders, all made of costly silks, each one hand-gilded by artisans in Paris."

"You *campaign* in poetry. You *govern* in prose."

Mario Cuomo

21

Technology

21st-century technology can be useful when it comes to planning a book, but I've not come across anything nearly as good for writing it as an old-fashioned pen. There's simply no e-quill.

The trouble with my new e-reader is that now I don't know how I'm supposed to judge a book.

My name is Justin Pickles but I write all my novels under the name of László Bíró. It's my pen name.

I'm stuck at home so I've just phoned the bookshop to confirm that they've got books about becoming a midwife. Good news. They can deliver.

I see that tomorrow is National Typewriter Awareness Day. I'll have to buy a ribbon.

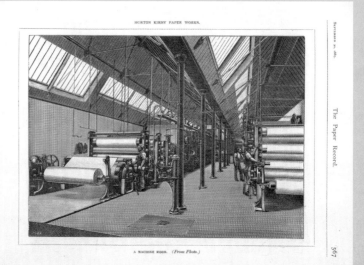

HORTON KIRBY PAPER WORKS.

A MACHINE ROOM. *(From Photo.)*

Customer: Could you give me some sound advice about listening to audiobooks please?
Bookseller: Not a problem. You need to buy some great earphones.

The machine room in a late Victorian paper factory (1887).

What does a pig use to write his autobiography?
A pig pen.

I learnt how to speed read last year so now I listen to audio books on fast forward.

Me: Could you play the Harry Potter audiobook?
DJ: No

My mum bought me *Internet Forums for Dummies* for Christmas. I hate to tell her, but I've already Reddit.

I'm reading *Dracula* in Braille and I'm sure something awful is just about to happen. I can feel it.

To tell the truth, it's taken me a while to learn how to read Braille and I've nearly given up a few times. It's been quite a bumpy ride.

Ages ago I worked for a specialist publishing company translating all of Pliny the Younger's letters into Braille. It feels like ancient history.

I've got to read what I'm buying online more carefully. I thought I was getting four Kindles but today Amazon delivered a Blu-ray of The Two Ronnies' Greatest Hits.

During lockdown I ran out of toilet paper. My wife suggested we should temporarily use pages from an old book which was fine for a bit, but made a horrible mess of my Kindle.

First dog, chewing on an audiobook CD: Urgghh! This tastes awful. **Second dog, chewing on a Kindle: Yes, this too. I've given it a chance but I prefer real books.**

First bookworm: Ever tried a Kindle?
Second bookworm: Only once, but it tasted quite funny.
First bookworm: Probably a joke book.

I regret buying that joke book for my Kindle now. It cracked it up.

I got so bored with my Tolstoy novel that I threw my Kindle across the room. It's wall and pieces now.

They've really gone high-tech in my local court. I refused to call the magistrates 'Your worships' and they downloaded the e-reader at me.

There's a mysterious Good Samaritan in my town who slips e-readers into people's shopping bags. He's performing random acts of kindleness.

I've got to stop these marathon reading sessions during the day and then long into the small hours. I'm burning the Kindle at both ends.

There are no books at my children's new pre-school, just e-readers. It's a kindlegarten.

I've written a new audiobook joke into my latest comedy set but I'm a bit worried people will say it's not a real joke.

I've been working on a new audiobook joke but I have to make sure I'm talking very clearly so that it's Audible.

I've lost the expensive new audiobook Mum got for Christmas. I'll probably never hear the end of it.

Plenty of writers don't shrink from posting on social media day and night about their new books. If they did, they'd be titchy now.

Novelist's wife: Can you explain why I always catch you playing Roblox rather than writing whenever I pop into your garden office?
Novelist: It's probably because your slippers don't make much noise.

Our love life was quite boring until we started reading e-books. Now our love has been rekindled.

Father Christmas didn't read my note properly and I just got lots of small pieces of wood in my sack this year.

Before the typewriter there must have been a prototypewriter.

22

The Editing Process

It's up to each and every one of us to proofread, otherwise the errorists will win.

Being a proofreader is quite easy as long as you know what to except.

I divide the world into those who prooofread and those who dont, so basically there are two typos.

Why are witches and wizards good editors?
They always spell check.

Why do proofreaders regularly vomit?
Typos make them [sic].

What do you get if you cross Marvin Gaye with a superb editor?
Textual healing.

23

Typography

Typography jokes differ from case to case.

There was a big fuss at church this morning when my godson was accidentally baptised Big Caslon. The priest used the wrong font.

I sent a strong reprimand to my co-workers about their failure to use proper formatting tools in documents. It was entirely justified.

I'd really like to tell you my font joke but I'm not bold enough.

What's the best typeface for a launch campaign?
Trebuchet.

What is a letterpress printer's favourite breakfast cereal?
Kern flakes.

I'm pretty picky about which fonts I get friendly with.
It has to be my type.

I'm always more likely to buy a book with the flag of Switzerland on the front cover. It's a big plus.

A tipsy Century Gothic and Frutiger Bold Condensed walk into a bar. Get out, says the barman, we don't want your type in here.

A man talks into a bar. You'll have to leave, says the landlord, we don't serve your typo in here.

I'm finding it hard to finish this book on chiropody. It's full of footnotes.

What did the first typeface dude at the beach say to the second typeface dude at the beach?
Grab your board, serif's up.

What is a typesetter's favourite chocolate snack?
M&M's.

What typeface do astrologists use?
Futura.

I'm not chubby, I'm just in bold.

A font goes on holiday to Italy and tries to make small talk at the Colosseum with a friendly-looking typeface. "Are you Roman?" he asks. "No," she says, "but I am Italic."

How do we know that a typographer designed the Leaning Tower of Pisa?
Because it was built in italics.

One of the reasons that fonts had a lot of trouble in Wild West towns was that they were often Sans Seriff.

I keep seeing childish jokes scribbled on the beach.
Must be comic sands.

Why do people instantly hate Helvetica?
It saves time.

Bob, a hyphen, and an Oxford comma walk into a bar. "I think there's space for both of you over there," says the barman.

'The Letter Makers Shop' from *High Street* written by JM Richards and illustrated by Eric Ravilious (1938).

24

Very Old Jokes

After he's spent all his allowance, a useless student has to sell his books for money. The next time he writes to his father he says: "You can congratulate me as my books are already supporting me!"

From *Philogelos*, the oldest surviving collection of jokes, compiled in ancient Greece during the 4th century AD, probably by Philagrius and Hierocles.

A moth ate words which seemed amazing to me, that a maggot could consume somebody's poem, a burglar in the dark... The thief was not at all smarter for swallowing these sentences.

From *The Exeter Book*, a late 10th-century collection of writings, most famous for its dozens of riddles including ones for which the answers are probably a bookcase and the Bible. The answer to this one is a bookworm.

When the poet Dante was living in exile in Siena, he was in a church examining his soul and privately preoccupied about something. A man approached him and asked various silly questions. "Ok, can you tell me which is the biggest animal?" replied Dante. "The elephant", said the man. "Well elephant," said Dante, "Leave me alone to consider things greater than your words and stop annoying me!"

From the *Facetiae* by Italian scholar Poggio Bracciolini, the first printed joke book, which appeared in 1470.

A scholler that had married a young wife, and was still at his Booke, preferring his serious study before dalliance with her. At length, as shee was one day wantoning whilst he was reading; Sir, saith shee, I could wish that I had beene made a Booke, for then you would still be poring upon me, and I should never, night nor day, be out of your fingers. So would I (Sweet-heart) answered he, so I might chuse what booke. When she demanded of him what booke he would wish her to be: Marry good wife (saith he) an Almanacke, for so I might have every year a new one.

***A Banquet of Jests* was a popular joke book first published in 1630 and regularly reprinted with updates in the following centuries. It is somewhat dubiously attributed to Archibald Armstrong, a jester at the courts of James VI and Charles I.**

I've had writer's block for ages now, so hopefully these new pens are a move in the write direction.

What do novelists do to confirm their contracts?
They sign on the plotted line.

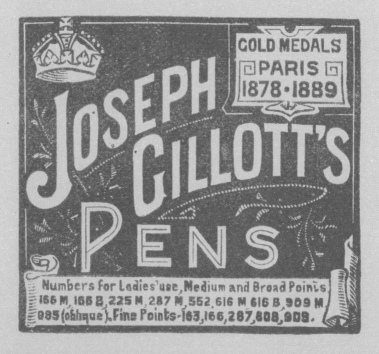

GOLD MEDALS
PARIS
1878 · 1889

JOSEPH GILLOTT'S
PENS

Numbers for Ladies'use, Medium and Broad Points
166 M, 166 B, 225 M, 287 M, 552, 616 M, 616 B, 909 M,
985 (obhque), Fine Points-163, 166, 287, 808, 909.

If you write a book about Chitty Chitty Bang Bang, would it be biography or autobiography?

I always buy notebooks with margins to write in.
I draw the line when it comes to blank ones.

I'd love to tell you my short story joke but it's still too long and I can't get the ending quite right.

I'm scribbling this short story down as fast as I can.
I'm binge inking.

All budding novelists have to get used to rejection early in their careers. It's a write of passage.

Did you hear the tale about the novelist who rented an office on the seventh floor of a tower block?
Then he rented one on the eighth floor, but that's another story.

My friend has just written a book arguing the case for atheism.
Now he's praying for it to be a bestseller.

Fuel shortages meant that unfortunately the recent author competition had to be cancelled.
It was a write-off.

My computer crashed and it swallowed all the drafts of my book on the history of itching. It looks like I'll have to start from scratch.

Who are the scariest authors?
Ghostwriters.

I'm not liking this novel about a church cemetery much. There's no plot.

Which monarch wrote the most books?
King Author.

My creative writing tutor at university always taught me that double negatives are a total no-no.

It was destiny that my history book would be published. It was bound to happen.

Why mustn't you write a book on an empty stomach?
Because it's much easier on paper.

My parrot's written a whole book of short stories.
That's astonishing. He must be a genius.
Not at all, he keeps mixing up 'affect' and 'effect'.

Vous allez être un grand savant, et moi je vais l'annoncer au monde

Some writers drink to steady their nerves. Sometimes they get so steady they can't move.

Why do you write so many different kinds of novels about double-agents?
Because variety is the life of spies.

Did you hear about the novelist whose earnings went into six figures?
Her husband and five children.

I'm getting worried about my novelist friend. Every time I go round to see him, he's rummaging around anxiously in all the waste paper bins. I think he's lost the plot.

Some writers leave a mark on the world. Sometimes it's just a stain.

Doctor, doctor, do you treat writers?
Yes, all the time.
Excellent, mine's a pint then.

His new novel is called *Nagb*. It's pretty controversial. In fact it's bang out of order.

Writer goes into a pub with a keyboard under his arm. "Get out!" shouts the barman. "We don't want your typing here."

To avoid stereotyping, writers should never write while their keyboards are plugged into their hi-fi speakers.

I finished writing my latest novel, parcelled it up at home, and stuck loads of stamps on it. But when I took it to the post office to send to my agent, the cashier weighed it and said: 'Sorry, but that's far too heavy. You'll have to put some more stamps on it." But I can't see how that's going to make it lighter.

What do gardeners and authors have in common?
They both like to work on their plots.

My author friend claims he "accidentally" glued himself to the manuscript of his autobiography. That's his story and he's sticking to it.

Did you hear about the author who was really pleased when he had to go to prison because it meant he could complete all his sentences.

On the other hand, did you see the court case about the author who was sued by his publisher for delivering a book that only had a dozen words in it?
The judge is considering a short sentence.

A 150-page novella with a 65-page introductory essay walks into a bar. The barman asks: "Why the long preface?"

What happened to the author who got his fingers mangled horribly in a freak typewriter accident?
He had to start writing in shorthand.

Definition of writer's block: when your so-called friends ghost you.

I've been to dozens of writers' retreats. Now I'm excellent at running away.

The author was in his mid-fifties when he wondered whether it was really worthwhile writing his series of novels about nurses having a tough time. It was a midwife crisis.

"Always read something that will make you look good if you die in the middle of it."

PJ O'Rourke

Schoolteacher: Okay, everybody, it's time for 'show and tell'.
Writer's child: You mean 'show, don't tell' surely?

I couldn't make up my mind so I just tossed a coin to choose a name for my new novel. So now it's called *Tails*.

What do you call somewhere only authors live?
A writer's block.

I'm taking the plunge and killing off several of the key characters in the book I'm writing. It's going to really pep up my autobiography.

I come from a long line of writers. The dole queue.

My girlfriend read the book I'm writing but complained that the protagonist was too whiny and self-obsessed. Bit rude to read my diary really.

The covers of my new series of novels are going to be decorated using the bottom of my trousers. It's a turn-up for the books.

My friend's a writer so for his birthday I'd like to give him something he's never had before. Like a job.

I've always wanted to write a whodunnit. Or <u>have</u> I?

My son's finally got his book coming out next week. I hope that puts him off eating another one.

My brother's a hardworking and popular man of letters.
That's great.
Yes, he's a postman.

A lady of the night sidles up to a worried-looking young man at the hotel bar, typing away furiously on his laptop. "I'll do anything for £100" she whispers in his ear. "Smashing," he replies, handing her his computer and the money. "This short story needs finishing by 9pm."

I've been working on my writer joke for a decade. I don't think I'm ever going to finish it.

I could tell you my writer joke, but it doesn't really work.

I did have a writer joke for you, but I got distracted by social media.

Daddy, you'll love my new boyfriend. He's a writer and he's so nice and polite.
That's great honey, but does he have any money?
Weird. He asked me the same question about you.

I had a writer joke but it's co-authored so I can only tell 50% of it.

What's the difference between a Christmas turkey and a writer?
The turkey can feed a family.

If a writer is born in Madrid, grows up in Tokyo, gives birth to children in Moscow, and dies in New York, what is she?
Dead.

I've just written a novel about three shipping tankers. One was full of red paint, one was full of brown paint, the third was full of blue paint. They crash together in middle of an ocean and the crews have to swim to shore through the wreckage. What's it called?
Marooned.

I made my money as a writer the old-fashioned way. I inherited it.

My first novel was my baby. It looked great from the outside but it took up all my time, destroyed my sleep, and took three years to get halfway decent.

I find him a very inspiring novelist. If he can get his books published, then anyone can.

I have a writer joke but I can only tell you some of it today and then I'll tell you the rest of it next September.

There's a new book out about the importance of grapes and how we should understand that they have feelings and needs too. It's all about raisin awareness.

After years of legal wranglings, Stephen Hawking's final unpublished book is finally coming out next year.
It's about time.

There's a great chapter in this book about film stunts which shows you the best way to fall down stairs. It's a step-by-step guide.

These two books contain the sum total of all human knowledge. What They Teach You at Harvard Business School *and* What They Don't Teach You at Harvard Business School.

Internet meme by Ryan Sabir.

A novelist bumped into a friend at a book launch party and began telling her about the success of his new novel. "Everybody loves it," he said. "The critics think it's marvellous, the bookshops can hardly keep up with demand, and it's a big hit among the book bloggers. They're saying I'm the new Dickens. I'm bound to win the Booker, at the very least. You can read all about me in the interview with *The Guardian* next week too. But Daisy, here I am, banging on about myself nonstop and I haven't even asked about you. So, what do *you* think of my novel?"

He was a writing prodigy. He wrote a novel at 10, a play at 11, and a book of poems at 12. Then at 12.30 he came downstairs for lunch.

My friend is writing a novel nearly every day. Nearly on Monday, nearly on Tuesday, nearly on Wednesday …

He writes really poor books about burglars. He's a criminal writer.

I've got the best unpublished novel ever written right here on my desk. The problem is that the author wants it back.

There's a writer in our road and I sometimes see him sticking pages of his work in a metal container and then putting them in a hole in his garden. I asked him today what was going on and he explained that it was just his can to bury tales.

I'm not sure about the proposed cover of my new book. My brain says yes, but my heart says no. Do your kidneys get the deciding vote?

Starving writer in his garrett: It's been so long since I've had any food that I've forgotten what it tastes like.
Stingy Landlord: Don't worry, it still tastes the same.

Is it hard to be a successful novella writer?
Yes, it's pretty tricky to cut a long story short.

Accountant: I've been looking at your income and I think it's time you stopped operating as a sole trader and became a company.
Writer: That's exciting! What kind? Public Limited company? Private company limited by shares? Limited Liability Partnership?
Accountant: No, a non-profit organisation.

Doctor, doctor, I can't stop myself writing novels about curtains.
Pull yourself together!

Did you write this novel in your garden office?
No, ink.

Prologue page to *The Works of Geoffrey Chaucer* designed and illustrated by Edward Burne-Jones and published by William Morris's Kelmscott Press (1896).

How did Farmer Giles win the Noel Prize for literature?
He was out standing in his field.

HERE BEGINNETH THE TALES OF CANTERBURY AND FIRST THE PROLOGUE THEREOF

WHAN THAT Aprille with his shoures soote
The droghte of March hath perced to the roote,
And bathed every veyne in swich licour,
Of which vertu engendred is the flour;
Whan Zephirus eek with his swete breeth
Inspired hath in every holt and heeth
The tendre croppes, and the yonge sonne
Hath in the Ram his halfe cours yronne,
And smale foweles maken melodye,
That slepen al the nyght with open eye,
So priketh hem nature in hir corages;
Thanne longen folk to goon on pilgrimages,
And palmeres for to seken straunge strondes,
To ferne halwes, kowthe in sondry londes;
And specially, from every shires ende
Of Engelond, to Caunterbury they wende,
The hooly blisful martir for to seke,
That hem hath holpen whan that they were
seeke.

Bifil that in that seson on a day,
In Southwerk at the Tabard as I lay,
Redy to wenden on my pilgrymage
To Caunterbury with ful devout corage,
At nyght were come into that hostelrye
Wel nyne and twenty in a compaignye,
Of sondry folk, by aventure yfalle
In felaweshipe, and pilgrimes were they alle,
That toward Caunterbury wolden ryde.

JO IN A VORTEX.

Every few weeks she would shut herself up in her room, put on her scribbling suit, and
"fall into a vortex," as she expressed it. — PAGE 44.

There's no way I can finish writing this book with this paté, cold chicken, grapes, crisps, and bottle of rosé tied to me.
Yes, you do seem to be hampered.

Why do writers call their desks a 'work station'?
Well, a bus station is where a bus stops, a train station is were a train stops, and …

Doctor: You've broken your fingers but we'll be able to sort them out.
Patient: **Will I be able to write a book once they're fixed?**
Doctor: Absolutely.
Patient: **Excellent, because I couldn't manage it before.**

Did you hear about the famous writer who couldn't face appearing at the Hay Festival because they wanted him to talk in a marquee in the morning and a yurt in the afternoon. It was two tents for him.

Teen 1: I'm very excited! Somebody's written a book about oxygen and magnesium!
Teen 2: **OMg!**

Why are atoms great at writing fiction?
They always make up everything!

What's it like to be a budding writer?
Well, it's hard to put into words.

Why are novelists better than poets?
They're prose.

Hey, I invented a new word in my latest novel!
Plagiarism.

Never leave alphabet soup cooking on the hob and go out of the kitchen. It could spell disaster.

My great-grandpa told me that when he was a toddler there were only 25 letters in the alphabet. He didn't know why.

Why are authors of dieting books so wealthy?
Because they're living off the fat of the land.

My book was written using a Ouija board.
You mean you used a ghost writer?

What kind of notebook does a dendrochronologist write in?
A tree-ring binder.

I'm writing a book about all the stuff I really should get round to doing in my life. It's my oughtobiography.

Why are writers always a bit chilly?
Because they're always surrounded by drafts.

What's the main cause of death for new writers?
Exposure.

I need to work on my pop-up book joke – it always falls a bit flat.

Why don't writers stare out of the window in the morning?
Because they'd have nothing to do in the afternoon.

Acknowledgements

Thanks to Zoe 'Shelf' Ross and Matthew 'Scallions' Perret. Also to everybody who has laughed politely at my hilarious jokes over the last 50 years, especially Paul Greatholder, Adrian Hill, Judith Carruthers, The Wednesday Night Snooker Club (The Vincinerator, The Judge, The Wizard, The Chalfont Champion, Bill, and Anthony), Sally 'Brigadoon' Davies, Emma Townshend, Jo Whyberd, Adam Parsons, Sarah '37' Salway, Chris Routledge, Mary de Sousa, and Uncle Wilco.

Illustration References

All references are British Library Shelfmarks and searchable on imagesonline.bl.uk

P.2 HS.74/1408 (10); **P.8** IB 344, f.350; **P.11** P.P.6004.glk p. 297; **P.12** royal ms 12 f xiii f021r; **P.15** 1870.b.3; **P.17** kh212894; **P.23** kh66987; **P.27** Cup.501.c.1; **P.30** 1876.f.22; **P.32** kh209595; **P.37** c03088-02; **P.39** C.39.k.15; **P.41** T00026-54; **P.44** 7942.dd.9; **P.52** F60049-39; **P.56** 8416.d.7(frontispiece); **Pp.60-61** 456.d.16 before a1; **P.66** 143.g.2; **P.69** 79.l.6-11 (volume 6 page 437); **P.75** L.45/2847; **P.76** 10604.g.10 volume I; **P.79** I.B.41735; **P.86** Simplicissimus 09/05/1896 page 5 issue 6; **P.89** 25/04/1896 p.5 issue 4; **P.98** c05914-03; **P.100** Royal 10 A. XIII; **P.107** 8234.ff.2 **P.110** 7942.dd.9. **P.113** 1457.k.1; **P.123** C.43.h.19; **P.124** 12844.m.8.